MIAMI PANIC

STORY OF

WAYNE COX

AND

THE SHENANDOAH RAPIST

WAYNE COX

Miami Panic
Story of Wayne Cox and the Shenandoah Rapist
by Wayne Cox

Printed in the United States of America

ISBN 9781498401708

Scripture quotations taken from the King James Version of the Bible.

www.xulonpress.com

ACKNOWLEDGMENTS

"For I know the plans I have for you",
Declares the Lord, "Plans to prosper you and
not to harm you, Plans to give you hope and
a future."

Jeremiah 29:11

As I hold this manuscript in my hands I know that it is with the Lord's guidance that I have been able to accomplish my book. I begin and end my days with him in prayer and hope that if I make a slight difference among his children, I can be at peace with myself.

I Thank You Lord:

For Your unconditional love and forgiveness for the times in which I have failed to do more for your glory.

For giving me the most magnificent mother a man can ask for. Rosaline P. Cox educated me with values, morals, and ethics. Her wisdom, strength, and support led me to be the man that I am today.

For placing in my life a beautiful, kind and gentle Grandmother, Clarice E. Spence. She willingly devoted to my brothers and myself all of her time and energy while my mother went out into the workforce to support her family. Although she is no longer with us and is truly missed, she will always remain in our hearts.

For my older brother, Gregory Cox: he has been a remarkable role model whose footsteps are difficult to follow. He has provided me with encouragement to believe in my dreams.

For my younger brother, Michael Cox: I became a more responsible individual because I knew he would find worth in my decisions. His enthusiasm and philosophical views have shown me a different perspective on life.

For my son, Christopher Cox: as I held him in my arms on the day he was born, I realized the true meaning of love. He has been a blessing in my life. I pray he continues on a righteous path as he begins a new journey after graduation. May Christopher learn to trust in you as I do. If he does, he will have nothing to fear, be capable of breaking any barrier, and become the leader he was born to be. Son, it is for you that I leave this small part of myself. One day my presence will be missing, but my spirit will live on in the pages of this book. Daddy loves you.

For my daughter, Christina Cox: I felt fortunate in having a son but never imagined I would be blessed a second time with a beautiful princess. She has brought endless joy and laughter.

For my special friend, Barbara N. Valdes: I remain indebted to her for her commendable determination, fortitude, perseverance and honesty.

For my friend James Berry Jr. from Just Right Photography: I am grateful for his generosity in providing the photographs.

For my dearest friends and family members who expressed their confidence in me throughout the writing process: I am honored by their kindness and willingness to give their time as you placed them in my presence at the perfect phase in my life.

And finally, for my readers: I pray that this book enlightens you to follow the word of the Lord. With him in our hearts, all things are possible.

Amen

TABLE OF CONTENTS

—⟶ოⅿ⟵—

Chapter One

THE AVERAGE DAYS

—⁓—

As with any other job, a law enforcement officer's routine duties can become a monotony that brings about unconsidered actions. Once an individual acclimates to his or her tasks, the daily activities seem to take on a role with few challenges, and soon are almost seen as dreary. Arresting the same types of offenders by using the exact strategies can become a burden that infuses boredom and causes one to ponder about the heroism that is commonly instilled in such a profession. With the public constantly criticizing the police in this country, individuals who have no respect or idea regarding the daily grind make an officer feel as if one has minimal value in their community. In addition to the lack of appreciation for their dedication to serve and protect a massive number of citizens, the absence of positive media interest can turn an officer into a disillusioned individual.

Wayne Cox was experiencing this dull-mindedness, and became disparaging about his chosen career. The daily operations of staking out drug dealers, drug addicts and speaking with informants led him to believe law enforcement was only a device used to circumvent the public into thinking there was some form of social control set into place. Wayne knew better than this, but could not stop rationalizing the value his activities essentially had for his community and society in general. Despite his endless efforts, there was always another criminal, an additional investigation and eventually a new arrest. Detective Cox did have moments that brought feelings of exhilaration, as he took pleasure in removing dangerous people from society who had no sense of respect for the lives of others, but these days were few and far in-between.

Detective Cox woke up daily at the break of dawn to the same undertakings as if some external force controlled his every movement. The day's events became monotonous from beginning to end establishing a sense of rigorous routine. Wayne began to view himself as a robot that was programmed to accomplish the day's responsibilities and never question its worth. Wayne's family noticed this, as he routinely discussed the drudgery with them repeating the same cop jargon over and over again but they did not have the heart to tell him. Simply put, Wayne was experiencing some sort of illness that could only be cured with a dose of excitement, and his current position was not providing him with

any medication. His partner becoming aware of the occupa-
tional unhappiness tried to slip in subliminal messages about
the noticed behavior. Wayne was caught in such a spiral of
boredom that every moment of his life was overcome with
the disdain that he was feeling. Needless to say his partner's
attempts were unsuccessful.

Wayne's lack of excitement also had a counterpart,
which was the shame he felt for enforcing the law upon
low-level offenders, especially when the majority of them
were minorities as himself. Being a Caribbean American,
Detective Cox found himself in a battle of contradiction yet
despite his remorseful feelings he had a job to do. There were
days he questioned the validity of his ethics as he fulfilled his
obligations to uphold the law in some areas that were populated largely by minorities. Seeing and arresting the same
offenders for delinquency that is considered to be non-vi-
olent or not a major threat to the public safety manifested
somewhat of a disgust within these communities. When
Wayne came into contact with some of the repeat offenders,
the value he had about his profession was staring back at
him in a disrespectful manner; similar to being slapped in
the face by the justice that he served. The revolving door of
the criminal justice system has a duality; officers feel rather
worthless when they implement justice and see the offender
participating in a similar behavior after taking some time to
intervene. How could they not? Wayne's dedication to provide the community with a safer environment for families

to prosper in had constantly been interrupted by the same offenders, offenders that were previously arrested by him and brought to justice.

The constant paperwork and court appearances were unpleasant procedures that made Wayne feel the day's events as a dreadful routine. This was certainly not what he envisioned when he began thinking about a career in law enforcement. As Wayne was never one to believe the media hype about police work, he was still baffled at how his job had turned into being an administrative assistant for the courts and jails combined. Predominantly the cases Wayne put all his energy into. He completed the paperwork with the most specific details, to then see the offenders who belonged inside of a cell getting away with their crimes due to some unusual legal technicality allowing them to walk out the front door of the court building without any justice attached. Angry and distressed, Wayne needed something to change; he went as far as contemplating proceeding a new career, but the innate spirit to serve and protect his community superseded the negative thoughts. The successful busts that he made, and the possibility of the next opportunity to keep the streets of the community safe kept his spirit going, but these days were few and far in-between.

One day Wayne had an epiphany, and believed that he had figured his problem of boredom out, but it was short lived which caused him to feel more disheartened. Being an educated man Wayne had done what most people would do when they realize they have become trapped in a mundane cyclone. Detective Cox started to change his routine, as well as his outlook on life's experiences. However, by being a reasonable person, and an individual who had been trained to pay attention to details, it was short-lived feeling trapped in the emptiness of a giant hole. Wayne explored with new foods, buying new clothes, and engaging in different leisure activities. He even worked up the courage to try different tactical approaches in his profession, but all of these strategies came to a crashing halt. Wayne had a noteworthy flash of rationalization, which was to determine the accurate reason for his problem—his boredom and skepticism.

The fear to look inside one's self and define the truth which lies within almost caused Wayne to throw in the towel completely. One morning, he stared in the mirror and asked, "What the hell happened to me?" He had no real answer, and could not even pinpoint when he started to think and feel insignificant. He felt heavy dragging himself around, acting as if nothing was wrong, which fed the already established misery allowing it to grow stronger. The "monkey on your back" phrase was no longer a saying in Wayne's life; it had become a reality which gave in to the misery as he became a world-class actor in a film titled "Happiness." A bomb of depression destroyed his lifelong goal of working in law enforcement. It seemed as if nothing could put the pieces back together until the boxing match in which Detective Cox fought within himself had entered the final round. Wayne's second wind set in; he was not going down without a fight. Wayne considered this his last resort. In his mind he knew it was the only chance he had to turn things around and forever leave the worthless pattern of living behind him.

CHAPTER TWO

DAY OF RECKONING

———◈◈◈———

September 22, 2002 was a day that Wayne Cox will never forget. It started out as any other day in the past. Wayne woke up and began his routine, he thought about what he could possibly bring to the community that day. This all changed when his phone buzzed on the dresser. Wayne darted to the phone. Detective Cox was aware that receiving an early call from work meant that a serious event had transpired. He had anxiously been waiting for this day to come. Upon answering the call and saying "Detective Cox" in the most serious tone he could conjure, Wayne learned of something that made all of his prior difficulties vanish without any hesitations. The person on the phone was one of Wayne's supervisors, and again, any call that occurred early in the morning meant that something had occurred in the community that required immediate attention. His supervisor told him that there had been a vicious crime committed in the Department's jurisdiction—the brutal rape of an eleven-year-old girl.

Wayne was revitalized, with anticipation over the investigation that he was about to launch. The drive to work was different. The adrenalin he felt and energy had gotten the best of him. Instead of listening to the same old music or radio shows, he found himself rushing through traffic with the volume on his radio completely down. He was ready to solve this crime and be the first officer to stand up for the community that he served. When he arrived at the police headquarters, other department staff noticed his anxiousness. His vitality immediately led him to the Supervisor who had called him. Wayne wanted to know all the details of the crime, but his energy was ceased by the lack of information on the suspect. In fact, the few clues could not give any detective considerable hope for solving the heinous crime. Despite the circumstances, Wayne remained optimistic and started working with the limited material that was available.

After speaking with numerous people and possible witnesses, Wayne noticed that he was dealing with something bigger than he had originally imagined; this was not some one-time event or a story that had been exaggerated by the victim and other people involved in the crime. A strange feeling overcame Wayne when he realized this. Though he wanted to feel the accomplishment and excitement of bringing a violent criminal to justice, he could not help but wonder if he would meet the challenge. Wariness began to plague his mind; this was the excitement he had been waiting for, yet the reality of possibly not being able to undertake the task made the days of mundanely and boredom more attractive. Wayne threw these belated thoughts away once he saw how the crime had impacted his community. This triggered a motivation to stop worrying about himself for once. There was more at stake than Wayne Cox's feelings; there was a crazed rapist amongst the community he cared for and the violent actions had to be put to justice—everyone was a possible victim. The citizens were in a panic: a Miami panic. No one felt safe, especially once the media began honing in on the crime. Police officers were distraught over the horrendous crime. Wayne was ready to change this and retain his newly found inspiration.

Once he began speaking to informants and possible suspects, Wayne felt a combination of heartache and desire for retribution. The media on his back challenged him in ways he never had been before. Rather than letting the pressure get to him, he now channeled it into doing his job with more passion; this revitalization was a new feeling for Wayne. Detective Cox knew that the crime had to be solved as the community's well-being was an element that was trying to be stolen. The constant barrage of questioning from the media was now a greater problem that it had originally been, mostly because the case was not advancing. Wayne and the numerous officers who were working on the case could not gather any great evidence. This made the police department, and especially Wayne, feel unserviceable. Despite the day-in, day-out of investigations, the law enforcement department was portrayed as inadequate. Even though he had experienced the scrutiny of law enforcement before, it was different this time—this was a very serious crime and could be the turning point or career-ending case for Wayne. This continued for weeks, and then something happened. The rapist victimized yet another innocent member of the community. It changed Wayne's attitude forever, and he now vowed to never feel sorry for himself again. His complaining days were over as his drive and motivation as a law enforcement officer began to peak again.

This offense offered some better clues as to what was going on inside of the rapist's mind, and gave Wayne a reestablished recognition of what he was dealing with; again, this was not some routine drug bust or low-level criminal. The town's panic centered on Wayne, and it was as if he could hear everyone's voices and fearful thoughts at once. Feeling anxious about his career choice was no longer an issue, as the second rape sparked an anger that Wayne had never felt before. More witnesses were coming forward this time, and there was now a sketch that could be made, and, in return, gave Detective Cox the image of the venomous man he was pursuing. One of the witnesses described the rapist as a Hispanic male of average height and with a mustache. More details allowed the sketch artist to present an image that would later be described as quite accurate, although the black and white image was not sufficient for Wayne. Detective Cox had negative experiences with witnesses who didn't give adequate descriptions, but knew that he had to take a chance to believe in the narrative given. It was this drawing that took all of the fear in the town, victims' worries, and media hype, and shaped them into what Wayne had called his day of reckoning.

Two rapes in a short period of time presented the idea to the entire country that the Miami-Dade area was not a safe location and was not managed well by law enforcement. News clips had nothing but negative things to say becoming even more ruthless after the second rape. According to Wayne, no one seemed to care about the victims; everything was about the crimes and the police department's inadequate performance. This prompted anger throughout the entire law enforcement community in the Miami-Dade area, and Wayne felt as if it was his personal responsibility to make sure that the offender was arrested as well as to put an end to the disparaging remarks that had descended upon the local community. In addition, Wayne and other law enforcers were taking heat from the citizens daily, often face-to-face. There were numerous days when residents in the Miami-Dade area subjected Wayne or one of his colleagues to harsh, sarcastic comments. The disgust that Wayne felt when these comments were made was unbearable, but there was nothing that could be done. The rapes had brought up the cliché idea that law enforcement focused on petty crimes and not the outrageous violent crimes that most people thought should have been the primary concentration of the police department.

The entire Miami-Dade area was full of fear, anger, and needless comments. Wayne found himself in a new tailspin. While he attempted to devote his full attention to the rapist, he could not help but feel the anxiety that citizens were exhibiting, but he also understood the hostility and why people were venting their frustrations aloud. Each hour that passed was concerning to the community not knowing when the rapist would assault an innocent victim. This allowed the media to deliver more negative hype and, in return, gave the residents motivation to ridicule law enforcement. Pressure was building, and it needed an escape. Wayne came up with a solution that he presented to his colleagues, but it was completely bypassed when another terrible thing happened. A third victim had emerged with grueling circumstances. The Shenandoah Rapist had no boundaries to his sinful acts which caused Wayne to erupt with vengeance and more passion to catch the perpetrator than any other occurrence in his life. As there had been many moments in Wayne's life that had renewed his motivation, this crime had put him over the edge, and Wayne's fury made him disregard his personal life in every fashion. His existence was all about investigating the case so that justice could be served; nothing else mattered to him. The third crime implicated a young female unaware that very morning that her innocence would be taken away, changing her life forever.

By this point, both local and national media outlets had descended upon the area, turning not only the Shenandoah district but most of the Miami-Dade metro area into a chaotic clutter of investigative journalist, cameramen and reporters. Constant interviews consisting of the same assumptions leaving too many questions unanswered made Wayne feel nauseating. Once again he noticed that most of the media attention had been geared towards presenting law enforcement as inadequate individuals. Unfortunately, not much time was devoted to the victims who had endured such a terrible form of suffering. Nonetheless, this latest offense brought more evidence and details into the case, as Wayne now had better information to use in the search for the offender who had been terrorizing the community. The offender's modus operandi and other traits were specifically becoming clearer allowing Detective Cox more insight into what this crazed maniac was up to. He perceived one thing in particular the offender was targeting the easiest prey he could find. The most recent victim produced a better description of the assailant, and the police now turned to different tactics. Rather than scouring the streets in marked patrol cars and cautioning people to walk with a friend, a massive clandestine approach was implemented. The basic patrols still existed, and the residents were still urged to familiarize themselves with safety information. However an additional plethora of undercover vehicles and police officers were deployed. Even off-duty officers were instructed to be on the lookout. Policing the entire Miami-Dade area, especially the Shenandoah district, became a twenty-four-hour a day job. Wayne began to think that the serial rapist would be captured before he could lay his grimy hands on another helpless victim. He told his informants that the police were not concerned with petty criminal activity or low-level drug dealing anymore, and simultaneously made deals with them so that if any information came to light, he would be notified immediately. Criminals Wayne had previously arrested were also willing to help. Even they did not condone the Shenandoah Rapist's violence.

Wayne continued to receive his tips and pieces of information, but none led to actually finding the rapist, nor did they add any significant intelligence to the investigation. Still, he felt better about his rapport with the community. Despite the unsolved horrific crimes, Wayne knew the people he had brought to justice were viewing his profession differently. The snarky comments and rude behavior by ignorant civilians became tolerable when he realized that his informants and past arrestees, who had more familiarity with the realities of crime solving, were on the same page as him. This also made him more determined to solve the case. The burden of knowing this malicious man was still looming and could not be suppressed, as Wayne fixated on making the victims' relief a reality. This put a veil over the media hype and the residents' hostility prompting Wayne to see them as insignificant leeches cashing in on despair.

As the investigation stilled, many of the law enforcement officers lost steam and let their rigorous surveillance falter, but this changed when the now-known Shenandoah Rapist struck again! The rape occurred in another Hispanic area, and the victim was another young female. The victim was raped in the one place that no person should have to worry or fear about being hurt—her home. Such a tragedy made everyone lose faith in the investigation. Every lead they had went nowhere. A psychopath was still at large contemplating his next sexual assault. Wayne became disillusioned and had again started to think that maybe this was his opportunity to retire and relieve himself of the stress that had stymied his well-being, but this changed when he met the young girl who was raped. Hearing the story and seeing the pain in her face gave him new ground to travel. He felt destined to bring this filthy malicious man to justice and provide some relief to the victims. It was difficult to get information from this victim because she was clearly suffering from post-traumatic stress and having trouble speaking about the awful situation— who could blame her?

Wayne used the young girl's powerful impression as inspiration to capture the beast. The only new lead that he had was the type of clothes the offender had been wearing, but this was useless since this man would most likely changed his clothes daily. Nevertheless, Wayne could not get over the fact that the Shenandoah Rapist had entered a house; he thought that neighbors in the community would notice such a thing, especially when awareness and fear were widespread. Where was everyone? How had they not noticed a man entering a home where he did not live? Was there no one that heard the screams or other noises? Was this guy that stealthy? Wayne tried to remove the questions and concentrate on moving forward in the investigation. He began to enter stores and community centers, asking for any information that would be useful in the manhunt. Yet again, nothing paid off. The Shenandoah Rapist was a ghost, and no one saw or heard anything different that was not already on file in the police department.

Several days went by before Wayne had noticed something that had yet to be discovered by any of his colleagues. The pattern of the Shenandoah Rapist was based on knowledge, but the attacks were still a kind of hit-and-run. So far, none of the rapes had been some random occurrence in a public or private place, and for some unknown reason, various criminal analysts and other specialists had not suggested this idea. In other words, Wayne noticed that the victims were raped during times that would be convenient for a sick-minded person like the Shenandoah Rapist. Wayne knew he had to have been stalking them prior to his vicious attacks, and that he was exploiting his victims' weaknesses the way a predator seeks out their target. This was verified when he received a phone call from a journalist who had asked him about the new case and how it was developing. Wayne started with his usual line about how he could go into the details of the case due to restrictions set forth by his department, but as he began to reassure the journalist that everything was being done to protect the victims and that the police were doing everything in their power to bring this terrible man to justice, the journalist interrupted. In a calm but somewhat resilient tone of voice, the reporter stated something that made Wayne's mind and body feel empty; he referred to a victim that Wayne had yet to hear about. A new rape had occurred.

Wayne abruptly hung the phone with little to add. His emptiness suddenly became rage. He could not believe that this was happening, and was baffled about what to do. After a few minutes of vengeful thinking, Wayne gathered himself and drove to his partner's house. Upon arriving, he found his partner and began speaking in an irate fashion. He could barely spew what he wanted to say. Once his partner was able to calm him down, the reason for Wayne's visit came out, and he found himself in tears for the first time in many years. There had been so much chaos, and too many people were full of fear; Wayne now felt he was partially to blame. The pressure of trying to rejuvenate his career while serving and protecting the public had turned into a personal stressor that could not be overcome with reassuring conversations. He had to find this maniac and put the misery that he, the victims, and other people were enduring. His partner offered many pieces of advice, but it was all nonsense to Wayne since he knew what the resolution to the problem was. Knowing that his partner could not provide it only brought more sadness, but one thing stuck out throughout the motivational lectures that his partner had been repeating over and over again. He advised Wayne to pay less attention to his surroundings and the media coverage, to detach himself from all of the hysteria and concentrate on doing his job. Wayne's brain turned back on, and he realized his partner was correct. He then stood up and gave his partner the handshake and eye-to-eye look that every law enforcement officer understood without any spoken words. Wayne realized that he had been centering his attention too much on the nonsense that had been going on. His mission was clear, and he would not bother with any more media hype. His feeling could be best described as heroic, as he did not care about anything except doing the right thing—bringing this scum to justice and allowing the Miami-Dade area to live without fear.

Wayne's motivation was gallant, and his manner of interviewing displayed this new perceptual change. He began to ask questions in a fashion that drew more information from the victims as well as the notion that he was doing every-thing he could to help them. The latest victim gave a better description of the man who was responsible for all of this wickedness in the Shenandoah area. Wayne had the face, but he could not find the predator anywhere, so he came up with a plan. He conjured up an investigative technique that was unprecedented, and even the top supervisors were impressed and thus gave the go-ahead for Wayne's new initiative. He planned to continue with the unmarked cars strategy, but he added plain-clothes officers to walk the streets as well. Second to this, he restructured the community involvement; by turning to block clubs and more community leaders as all-seeing eyes, Wayne was able to gather much more knowl-edge about suspicious behavior and conspicuous persons faster than before. However, the leads still ended up with nothing that helped bring the Shenandoah Rapist to justice.

At this point, Wayne was astonished. This averaged-sized Hispanic male was a ghost and seemed to specialize not only in rape, but also in making law enforcement look unskilled. The buffoonery was again merited when another person became a victim; the rapist had swooped down from his evil dwelling and claimed a sixth sadistic notch in his belt. This time it was an elderly woman. Wayne was as furious as can be, as well as con-fused about how this could occur during such a strong effort of watchman-style policing. Additionally, he could not help thinking about which crime was worse: attacks on juveniles, or horrific violence against someone's grandmother. He finally rested on the idea that neither crime was superior, and that this entire saga had spun out-of-control. It was time for Wayne to do something that he never thought he would during his career, something that he had always reserved for his off-duty life. He prayed that night, and asked his higher power to help him end this madness and bring relief to the residents in the Shenandoah district and entire Miami-Dade area, including himself.

After looking for assistance that night Wayne found the needed alleviation that he was searching for. He felt calm, which encouraged him to continue with an undoubted diligence in the investigation. He knew that he could not revert to self-loathing and pity; the victims and residents needed his mind to not be distorted. The serial rapist was still free, and something had to happen fast. Wayne thought that if nothing for the better occurred, even his faith would have to be questioned, a strong conviction that he never thought would have to be debated. Relentless questioning and patrols were conducted, and the description of the vehicle, a dark green Mazda, could not be found. Wayne found this to be unusual, as most of his other investigations always led to him finding vehicles with the same description everywhere, yet for some reason, this was not happening. The car seemed to be nonexistent, as well as a vehicle that no one else seemed to be driving; it was as if God was playing tricks on Wayne.

Investigating a ghost and a fictitious vehicle became extremely annoying. From prior experience, Wayne knew that something had to be going on. He started to look at stolen vehicles within the entire Miami-Dade area; the research went nowhere. His next step was searching the Department of Motor Vehicles registry, but even this did not narrow his investigation down to a single person or residence. The number of dark green Mazda's was overwhelming, and again, brought Wayne confusing thoughts—why could he not locate this vehicle then? Law enforcement had done everything, they searched high-and-low at train stations, airports, cheap motels, and even under highway overpasses, but nothing was coming up. This Hispanic mustached male had to have left the area and returned only to victimize an innocent female; it was beyond Wayne's comprehension that any other possibility could be imagined. His mind began to shift from the motivation that he promised himself to the doubtful thoughts again, but this all changed when he heard the news that another young girl had been raped—a seventh victim.

Filled with rage and hate for the first time in his life, Wayne looked at the young girl and did something that he had never done before. The interviewing techniques had such a sympathetic role that the young girl appeared to not even be in shock. She supplied Wayne and other police officers with details that no other victim could provide. The facial details, height, clothes, smell, things he said, and how he went about the ultimate sin of rape. Wayne was astonished at how this young girl could remember so much and not be struck by heavy grief. New facts were gained, and Wayne and his colleagues returned to the streets to solve the crime of the century. Again, Wayne had no tolerance for questions from the media or citizen flack; his mind was set on ending this once and for all. The investigation started to take heat from federal authorities, and Wayne knew that if something did not happen soon, his diligence would be a giant waste of time. Once the federal authorities took over, the investigations by Wayne and other law enforcement officers would be greatly diminished. Basically, they would be turned into assisting patrol units for the federal authorities and other national investigators. This is not what Wayne or anyone else wanted.

During a span of approximately a year, the Shenandoah Rapist had raped seven females, ranging from ages eleven to seventy-nine, but nothing was solved, or even close to being solved. The Rapist had entered people's sanctuaries and exploited not only their peace of mind, but also their bodies. Wayne knew that an evil being had risen in his community, and he was desperately trying not to lose it and leave without doing what he could to restore the community to a safer state. This was a difficult challenge, and the community and media had been making law enforcement look almost as bad as the Rapist himself. This all changed not long after the last attack, but Wayne did not feel the joy he thought he would. The media shifted from presenting law enforcement as the criminals to the heroes they were referred to prior to these terrible incidents.

CHAPTER THREE

THE RUSH

—⁓—

The task of overcoming his disheartening feelings was short-lived when Wayne looked back at all the turmoil that had occurred within the year. He spent the majority of the time investigating and thinking about the crimes. Not much of his time was devoted to his family and friends, and when it was, his mind was still focused on the investigation. This all changed when Wayne's phone buzzed, during a shift he felt would lead him to this evil psychopath; but his optimism was crushed by the voice on the other end of the phone. He knew immediately by the tone that it was not another rape, but something different, as he could tell by the hesitation and stuttering that had commenced. The news was mindboggling as Wayne learned the vehicle that the Shenandoah Rapist was using had been recognized and pulled over. After a quick interval of questioning, as well as a DNA sample, it was determined that the madman had finally been deprived of his freedom. It was true, the psychopath that Wayne had been chasing and putting his whole life on hold for had been caught through a basic traffic stop. A sense of mixed emotions rushed through Wayne as he felt compelled to immediately hurry to the station and exhaust his energy in attempting to rationalize why the officers that made the arrest didn't call him sooner. Wayne was once again feeling disappointed, this time going against his religious morals by saying the Lord's name in vain.

Except for the arresting officers, no one else was able to speak to or look at the serial rapist, which made the last year of Wayne's life seem purposeless. Everything he learned was through the media and locker-room chats with other law enforcers. The name was one that could not be forgotten, a double initial name that stuck out like a sore thumb—Reynaldo Rapalo. Wayne tried to imagine if he had encountered Rapalo in his previous investigative excursions, but knew this was not true. Rapalo was an offender who had been flying under the police radar. Rapalo's clandestineness made Wayne irritated; thoughts about whether he was doing his job properly entered his mind. He reassured himself that this was not true but was trapped in a world controlled by the criminal he did not arrest. Jargon became a second language for Wayne; all he did for the first few days after the arrest was glare at the newsreels that made headline patrol officers look like the finest law enforcers in the entire Miami-Dade area.

This stubbornness and resentful thinking lasted for several weeks after Rapalo was arrested and eventually arraigned. At last, the community was at peace, and Wayne found himself observing the return of communal happiness. Due to these extensive observations, he decided not to let his anger get to him. Because of this new enlightenment, Wayne found the happiness that he had wanted for so long. Even though he was not the officer responsible for the arrest, he knew that he had participated in a massive manhunt that ended peacefully. The Shenandoah district, as well as the whole Miami-Dade area, had now become safer because of the diligent work of law enforcement, and Wayne knew that he had been part of the reason for this newly rejuvenated harmony. He felt that it was time to move on and cut himself some slack. Moreover, his family and friends appreciated the fact that he had made this commitment, and Wayne definitely felt relieved with his career and personal life.

Many things started to work out for Wayne as he contributed this to the idea that Rapalo was finally at home, where he should be—in jail. Also, Wayne's relationship with his children grew to a level that was exhilarating for him. There was not a day that passed when he did not look at his children and thank God that they were safe, especially his daughter; this took his mind away from the rush that he had endured for an entire year of his life. The sky opened up, and rays of sunshine constantly poured into the Cox household; nothing could penetrate this joy that had entered his life. Of course, this bliss had carried over into his professional career, and Wayne now received compliments not only from his colleagues at work, but also the offenders that he was investigating and arresting. Not long after the Rapalo arrest, Wayne became known in the criminal underworld as one of the most respectful and fair police officers. This had an incalculable payoff for him; he was now not only making his job a lot safer for himself and his partner, but his reputation had grown so much that he had become a semi-celebrity in some neighborhoods. People would shout to him as he drove through specific areas, as well as calling the police station and asking to be picked up on warrants by "that cop who is cool, Cox or something." Wayne was a walking public relations movement that every law enforcement agency dreamed of, and the best part, at least in Wayne's opinion, was that he was getting attention and praise for a profession he was passionate about. How many people can say they truly love what they do for a living while making a difference within the community?

Contemplations of promotions or a public office position began to circle in his mind. He thought that even if he were offered a position which would require a professional change, he would remain active at street level so that he could continue on with his new vision. Immersed in the heightened delusions of the high life, Wayne now felt obligated to do more than police work and provide a safe community to the residents of the Miami area via law enforcement. He started to look into youth and victim's rights organizations; he thought that this form of volunteering would surely help others understand how great things could be achieved with perseverance. The optimistic approach continued for several weeks consequently being the best he had felt within the past year, and he did not want it to end, but even good things dissipate with time—and he was correct.

About four weeks after the arrest of Shenandoah's worst criminal, Wayne started to have unusual feelings that slowly impeded his happiness. The first thoughts were related to the victims, their families and how they were most likely still suffering. This troubled him so much that he began wondering about Rapalo's thoughts; was he feeling any remorse or sensitivity toward the people he had brutalized. What was going on in this terrorist's mind while he lay in bed at night?

Did he even understand the substantial damage he had caused with so many lives? Wayne shook his head every time these thoughts penetrated his brain, and somehow was still able to ride the tail end of his conquering approach without letting these pessimistic images completely take over. An exuberant amount of joy had entered his life, and Wayne did not want it to cease because of cynical thoughts. The fact remained that Rapalo was behind bars and could no longer hurt any innocent people; this fact superseded any bitterness or terrible rational. Similarly, he refused to return to a lifestyle that he had prior to the serial rapes, and wanted the relationship with his children to continue prospering. Regression was not an option Wayne would ever entertain since it would affect the people he loved the most. It also seemed as if the rest of the community, including law enforcement, had moved past these horrific tragedies, and Wayne did not want to be the person who was adamant to live in the past. In his new school of thought, Wayne would rather keep his positive frame of mind than to dwell on the negativity he was once plagued with. The fact remained that his passion and dedication to finding Rapalo had ended because of a very simple task, as well as not directly involving him; the disappointment seemed to have more weight than he ever imagined.

Optimism ended on a weekend when Wayne and his children planned to spend time together. Both his son and daughter asked him if he would put in the effort to keep on spending more time with them; obviously the answer was rooted in the typical elements of proper parenting, and Wayne assured his kids that this would not be a problem, not now, or ever. This bonding helped Wayne realize that his career was not of primary importance in his life, and that his family, particularly his children, were the seeds for everlasting happiness. Additionally, he found that by having such a positive attitude, other doors began to not only open for him, but also for the people around him. Wayne took this as a sign from his higher power as well, and then reconfigured his thoughts about what else he could implement into his life so that the prosperity could carry on and become even greater.

Other than the participation of various community organizations, Wayne started to think about setting up his own foundation and, in turn, helping people any way that he could. His family and friends loved the idea, and he soon began deciding what types of civil services he wanted to concentrate on. However, all of these pure actions of harmony were once again trampled upon, and Wayne knew that this time that he could not push the negativity away—this was something that could be not ignored. After a long day of work and taking his children out for ice cream, Wayne found himself on his recliner, watching the local news before he planned to go to bed. Everything was normal at first. He imagined that the reporters would communicate information that had little significance and then transition into the weather for the following week, but this is not what happened at all.

The special report music and big shiny lettering immediately caught his attention. This intrigued Wayne, because not much had occurred since the Rapalo arrest. His investigative senses also came alive and made him perk up in his chair to no longer feel the exhaustion from the lengthy day of activities. Wayne's common sense got the best of him as he awaited this so-called late-breaking news. He was working all day and had not heard anything, nor had anyone he encountered mentioned to him. Therefore, this Special Report was an event that had recently occurred.

On this particular evening, Wayne learned that his once-arch nemesis, Reynaldo Rapalo, had entered his life once again, and this time in an extremely embarrassing fashion. Tuesday, December 20th was another day that Wayne would never forget. There was nothing like this news that made him so stunned; he was silent with a combination of amazement, confusion, and anger—Reynaldo Rapalo had been able to escape from jail and had not yet been found. The Shenandoah Rapist had done it again. This crazed lunatic had caused another massive Miami panic.

Wayne thought he was dreaming. The way that Rapalo had foiled law enforcement had once again made them appear to look like amateurs. At some point during his confinement, Rapalo was able to acquire crude tools, break through a jailhouse vent, and shimmy down with a rope made of extra sheets. He was also able to recruit another sex offender. It was later learned that Rapalo used this man as a decoy, which meant that he was not the typical dumb criminal. Rapalo had more tricks up his sleeves then many investigators imagined. Wayne sprung up from his chair, which he was barely sitting on at this point, and called his partner to see if he had heard the news.

The investigation and search were already underway.
One of Wayne's supervisors had stated during the interview

on television that every transportation hub was being staked out, and that each person who had any contact with Rapalo during his short incarceration was being relentlessly questioned. However, Wayne thought that it was too late, and Rapalo had made it out of the area and was already somewhere else, in the midst of planning his next attack. This thought pushed Wayne's rage to a higher level, as he knew that if this was true, he would not be able to be a part of this new manhunt, and, even worse, more innocent people would become victims. Wayne could not fathom this as he drove to the scene to meet with his sergeant.

Pictures and crime scene sketches were the first items that Wayne viewed, followed by visitor statements, but Wayne knew that Rapalo would not be in contact with any of his relatives anymore since the event had become a national headline. Rapalo was on his own. Wayne could not comprehend one idea that his mind fostered: how could Rapalo not be found quickly? Everyone in the country now knew who this guy was, and with the crimes he had committed, there should be ongoing tips coming in to the department. A strange chill entered the Miami-Dade area, and Wayne began to contemplate the event as a malevolent hand of faith — how else could this be explained?

Overall, Wayne had gone from questioning his life choices to embarking with newfound pride, and then back to thinking that he was part of a challenge that God, for some strange reason, decided to provide him with. Reynaldo Rapalo was again the only element in his life he was focusing on, and because of this, Wayne realized that the joy he had been parading around with had a false sense of worth. Motivation took hold as Wayne found himself in a mindset that detectives frequently apply, that of complete focus as this case had to be solved, as quickly as possible by him.

CHAPTER FOUR

FALSE PRIDE

—⦿—

R apalo had given Wayne a false pride, and this was the biggest insult Wayne could imagine. A terrible form of a human being had taken his sanity, given him joy, and then snatched him away from his family and friends once more. Something had to be conquered, and the only thing that Wayne could think of that would stop this rollercoaster of emotions was for him to capture this maniac. Once again, Reynaldo Rapalo, The Shenandoah Rapist, was the only thing Wayne concentrated on. Moreover, the manhunt took not only his pride, but the integrity and diligence of every law enforcement professional in the Miami-Dade area. Everyone was so shocked that they were not sure how to even go about the investigation, and Wayne now had a perceptional commonality with every one of his law enforcement colleagues—even the people he did not know.

After the first few hectic days, it seemed that the same strategies were being deployed. Wayne knew that this was complete madness, but what else could be done? The transportation hubs were being staked out, not one investigator found any bus or plane tickets in Rapalo's name, and no stolen cars or other crimes that described someone with Rapalo-like characteristics were reported. Wayne, as well as everyone else, was starting to think that Rapalo had gotten the best of them, and was now out of the country, possibly stalking his next crime victim. If this was true, then Wayne was dealing with more than a false sense of pride; he was also dealing with a permanent falsified happiness. This plagued his mind so much that he found himself thinking about what his future would be like if he did not come across Rapalo. Wayne was baffled about what to do, so he did the one thing that he knew would help. He prayed to God, and repeated the phrase, "God can do great things for people who believe." This calmed Wayne, and he knew that this was a case that was larger than life. It had to be a sign from his higher power. He knew that someone, or something, had put him in this situation, and it was not Rapalo or some other person he had met. God had deliberately done this to Wayne. There was a motive that needed to be discovered, but Wayne still thought that he had to catch this predator, and that if he did not, his life may not turn out as he expected. His desire to prove his faith and figure out this divine enigma became his primary motivation. Wayne launched a personal investigation that was now faith-based. Because of this, his prior skepticism miraculously disappeared.

He could feel the presence of a third party, and it was not the essence of evil via Rapalo. Wayne and his partner became crusaders for the Shenandoah area, and, in turn, conducted themselves with a diligence that was similar to that which they showed when they were on twenty-four-hour surveillance. Each minute consisted of detailed observations, and they consumed massive amounts of caffeine and processed food to keep their awareness heightened. This went on for several days, and the two only stopped briefly to acquire some authentic nutrition and pass lame jokes back and forth to pass the time and endure the mundanely in which they were invested. Wayne looked to these small moments of informality for freedom from his constant thinking, and he soon realized that even with the terrible tragedies that had occurred, these moments made everything in his life worthwhile. One particular evening, Wayne and his partner were sharing the wealth of humor and pizza, but the laughter and small talk ended when their radio conveyed a message that would forever change their lives. A tip had come in that suggested a person who looked like Rapalo was spotted in the area where Wayne and his partner were. A surge of energy helped them hurry to the location where the tip had suggested this person would be. Upon arriving, they found the person who matched the description and immediately converged on him. It was unclear whether they were speaking to Rapalo, but Wayne's third party seemed to kick in more so than ever before; something, or someone, was telling him that this was the devil he had been looking for the last year of his life. However, because of the complaints about prior investigation tactics by human rights groups, he had to remain calm and professional. Zealousness was currently frowned on by the brass that Wayne and his colleagues worked with; everything had to be procedural and by-the-book.

The interview started with the basic questions of identification and reasons for being in the area, but they were perverted by the "No hablo" replies. By being in an area that was predominately populated by Hispanic people, Wayne started to begin to think that this was true and that this man was no evil wrongdoer, but rather an immigrant who spoke little English and only shared Rapalo's physical features. The fact remained the every other tip that had entered the Hotline had turned out to be frivolous. Wayne's professional training started to kick in again when he noticed the insecure voice inflections and body language that this man was displaying; something was not right, and now the third party started to emanate even more when Wayne recognized this behavior. Something, or someone, was telling him that there was something quite odd about this man and the situation in which Wayne and his partner found themselves. These paranoid thoughts were confirmed once something quite unexpected happened: the suspect darted off and started a foot chase that was unprecedented for Wayne. Now he knew that something was wrong. Wayne's extra sense kicked in, and he found his body moving without much prior thought. A Higher Power had given him the actions that were necessary to chase this man down, and during the foot pursuit Wayne noticed something that was marvelous and strange as well. It appeared that the night wasn't as dark, and that a light had shone down from above and given Wayne an energy that was not of this earth. The chase gave Wayne simultaneous thoughts. He had never done this before; usually his mind was shut off, and the only thing that he concentrated on was the pursuit. This time, it was different.

His feet felt tingly, and his eyes were responsive more than they had been during any other foot pursuits. Wayne noticed all of these unworldly kinesics, but his body was still following this man who had started the chase. Each obstacle that Wayne came across was no challenge, as he found himself to have decathlon-like abilities: every turn, garbage can, fence, or moving object was easily avoided. The pursuit was reaching a finish line that would put Wayne in first place. As he became closer to this amateur runner, Wayne's senses became heightened, and this third party that put all of these super-human abilities into him cast one more spell. Wayne was struck with the reality that this was the man who had been terrorizing Little Havana and the Shenandoah area. Even though it was not yet confirmed through science and he was still engaged in the chase, Wayne had somehow connected the acquired senses to the fact that this was the moment that he had been working toward for the past year. As he got closer and closer, Wayne knew that his faith was now unquestionable, and the few more steps that were in front of him were all that he needed to end the previous challenges to his faith. Then it happened. A divine intervention allowed Wayne to come within an arm's length of the Shenandoah Rapist.

Unconsciously, his arm raised up and reached out to grab the so-called immigrant's greasy t-shirt. When Wayne felt the cloth, a cold chill entered through his fingertips. From this point on, there was no denying that God had given Wayne this mission to secure the evil that had entered his community, but he was not close enough to subdue the beast that he had been constantly thinking about for over the past year. More ground needed to be gained, and it appeared to Wayne that this cold chill had counteracted the divineness that he had procured. The cold chill was more than a simple breeze. It was an evil energy that hindered the good that had entered Wayne's body and mind. Wayne knew this because his natural lung capacity and physical endurance returned. His footing started to slip, and the distance between him and the unusual evil was growing. Moreover, the light that had somehow manifested began to dim, and Wayne started to think that his higher power was about to be outdone by the creature ahead of him. Wayne could not help but realize that as this pursuit continued, his mind was full of deep thoughts, and that his body's movement was not being hindered even though the chase seemed to be turning out in Rapalo's favor and Wayne found himself breathing heavily and sweating for the first time. All of this changed in an instant; Wayne remembered something that would change this chase, and life, forever.

By noticing the ability to think and chase a man simultaneously, Wayne turned to the one thing that had given him diligence a few days before this encounter with the rapist. He quickly looked up at the sky and recited his prayer that he used to regain his confidence before this night; "God can do great things for people who believe." Before the last word was uttered, Wayne felt another surge of power come upon him, and he was no longer tired or clumsy-footed. The light that was before shone brighter, and Wayne was now getting closer to Rapalo. Again, he was within an arm's reach of the person who had tormented an entire community, and with a few more rapid steps, Wayne felt his arm begin to rise without any of his authority. This time when his fingertips touched Rapalo's t-shirt, the cold chill quickly became overwhelmed by a warming sensation that allowed him to finally tackle this maniac to the ground.

A tussle quickly emerged, and Wayne felt the wrath of this evil spirit more than via a cold chill in his fingertips. Something was not right, as they both were wrestling for control of each other. Evil and terrible images began to enter Wayne's mind, and he was able to see the true evil that the entire Miami-Dade area encountered in his mind. Snapshots of the victims' faces as Rapalo committed his rapes entered Wayne's mind, and this was so overwhelming that the cold chill began to take over the divine warmness that Wayne had been given. However, Wayne kept repeating the small prayer that he had made, and a blend of warm and cold sensations surged throughout his body. Not only was Wayne in a fight with the man he had been chasing for over a year, but he had become a conduit between good and evil; to Wayne, this felt like an eternity. Swapping between the cold and warm sensations was exhausting, but Wayne kept on repeating his prayer: "God can do great things for people who believe." Each time Wayne said this, his voice became louder and the power that had been put into him became stronger. Finally, because of the constant repeating of the prayer, the cold chills and terrible images were over. Wayne realized that his partner and other colleagues had arrived at the wrestling match and offered help to put Rapalo in handcuffs.

After briefly resisting of arrest, Rapalo was finally subdued and put into the back of a squad car. Wayne's humanness came back, and he now felt the sweat and gasps for air that every normal human being endures when such running and bodily engagement occur. He was exhausted, scratched, and bruised all over his body, but he knew that this long era of terror was finally over; there was no way that Rapalo would be able to escape from law enforcement this time. Out of the divine interventions and unusual course of actions that occurred, Wayne noticed one thing that he found to be truly disturbing. That is, when he looked into Rapalo's face while he was sitting in the patrol unit, he noticed that this subhuman species was smiling, and not hanging his head or hiding his face like every other criminal that Wayne had encountered. Wayne was reassured that this was no simple case, and that something had led him to this investigation.

It was later confirmed that the man, or evil spirit, who was detained and arrested was certainly Reynaldo Rapalo, and with an infallible DNA test, there was also no doubt that the person responsible for the rapes that had ensued throughout the year was in fact sitting in the police station. A year of terror had overwhelmed the Shenandoah area, and then reemerged after Rapalo managed to escape his confinement. The victims, and entire community, were breathing more calmly and now able to not fear their own neighborhoods. Each victim was personally contacted and told that Rapalo was finally being put to justice, and that they would never have to fear this man again. Also, law enforcement all over the nation celebrated this day with more passion than ever before. It was a unique day in the Miami-Dade area, and Wayne now felt the pressure and stress finally going away. He was asked to speak to the media, and, in turn, graciously accepted the contract; as he knew that this was the time to let his community as well as his professional and personal families share the wealth of reestablished trust in the neighborhood they lived in.

CHAPTER FIVE

REESTABLISHED PUBLIC TRUST

———

W ayne gathered with his partner in his supervisor's office and they went over the plan on how to address the media. It was nothing spectacular, and the conversation was mostly centered on ethics, how to properly represent the department, and how to speak. Wayne had no problem with this because he was tingling from head to toe, and he realized that this interview was going to be nationally televised; it was imperative that he not make an ass of himself. The media had converged in front of Wayne's headquarters. It looked like a tailgate party before a National Football League game; there was a plethora of tents, vans, and people who were milling around with cameras and microphones, constantly flipping through small notebooks, and touching up their faces and attire. Wayne was somewhat in shock because he had hated the circus that had assembled before his second home, and now he was about to stand before them and accept their arrival in the Miami-Dade area. It was expected that he answer basic questions and not go into detail about the victims' names or current state. It was also suggested that Wayne and his partner not take sole credit for the capture of Rapalo, and imply that they were only doing what any other law enforcement officer would do in the situation. Wayne had no dilemmas about this and had planned to mention some team-based effort anyway.

CRIME

SPOTLIGHT: Miami-Dade detectives Alcides Velez and Wayne Cox enjoy Monday's announcement of their capture of the man accused of being the Shenandoah rapist. 'I've arrested many people in my career. This one was closer to home,' Cox said Tuesday.

MARICE COHN BAND
MIAMI HERALD STAFF

Detectives have quite a story to tell, but moms hear it first

It was dark out when the interviewing commenced, and the combination of the lights on the vehicles and cameras made the parking lot glisten like a New Year's celebration. Wayne was starting to feel nervous again because he had never been the focus of so many eyes before; all of the prior

encounters with the media were smalltime local media outlets that were only interested in quick facts to fill time during
the evening broadcasts. However, Wayne knew that he had
to stand tall and speak clearly in order to send a message
to not only to the Miami-Dade residents, but also the entire
nation. It was going to be a day when law enforcement could
bounce back from all of the terrible attention that that had
been received in the media throughout everyone's careers.
This evening would reestablish trust with the public, and
it was going to be made very clear that law enforcement
were here to serve and protect, particularly in the Miami-
Dade area.

The lead investigators, top-level supervisors, and other
important law enforcers were all lined up on one side, and
the media was on the other side. It looked like a scene from
The Outsiders, but this was no gang fight, and Wayne found
himself huddled between all of these important police officials for the first time in his life. He liked the attention of
being meshed with the people he had taken orders from over
the many years that he had worked in field. One by one, each
person took their turn at the podium and answered questions
that seemed to be quite redundant. Each person expounded
on how this could not have occurred without the dedication and teamwork of every participant. Wayne was called
up next by a top-level supervisor, and introduced as one of
the detectives who captured Rapalo. The questions he entertained were very simple, and he found himself doing the

routine of thanking his partner and other professional colleagues, but one statement made Wayne stand out from all of the other interviews. That is, Wayne not only thanked God for the ability to deal with this unusual situation, but also the public for hanging in there and helping out with all of the calls and patience that took place over the last year. This made Wayne look like the most concerned individual who was standing on the law enforcement side, and the media ate it up like a starving person on Thanksgiving Day. Second to this, it gave people great perceptions of him all over the United States, and the residents surely enjoyed this rhetoric as well.

The day after the interview, Wayne and his partner were dumbfounded about what to do. The entire year had been devoted to catching Rapalo, and now that he was behind bars for good, the normal investigative work seemed to not be so appealing. Wayne and his partner were also enjoying the residents' cheering them on and positive compliments as they worked; the rude and very visible cynicism had vanished, and was now replaced with respect and encouragement. Because of this, Wayne attributed the lack of investigation, and crimes in general, to this respect for law enforcement and overall community. It appeared that criminal activity had ceased momentarily after Rapalo had been arrested and the interviews took place. Public trust was at the highest level that Wayne had ever seen. He was starting to think that if this carried on then he, and the many others, may not have a full-time job, but this was something that Wayne was all right with. If the streets and people were safe, then Wayne was all right with this lack of work.

Joyous feelings and overall happiness were also very apparent in Wayne's professional life. Many people who he once deemed miserable and angry became elated with the fact that such a paradigm had emerged. The work environment flourished because of this overall attitude. Every call, report, or complaint was handled in a manner that was the definition of public servility. The blue shield philosophy seemed to not be impenetrable, and not many people opposed this rendition of law enforcement at the current moment. Every day appeared to bring emotions like a birthday celebration, and with the minor disputes that were occurring, the rapport between the public and police officers had much more positive results and more reasonable approaches. The Miami-Dade area had become the epitome of ethical procedures and merriness that is only seen in Hollywood movies; the entire area emanated a passion for positive change and true diligence in protecting the people.

Wayne was now back to his Dali Llama mentality, and he felt that this time it would last longer than expected since there was an enormous amount of collective efficacy going on. His job turned into hours that were not full of paranoia or hate toward criminals, and he and his partner now viewed the world in a different light. Additionally, Wayne was able to see the beauty that every person offered to the world, since not many people had an evil and violent spirit like Rapalo. He dealt with the few criminal matters he encountered in a fashion that was similar to how an equal rights activist would portray themselves in society. Secondly, rather than the public not cooperating with Wayne and his partner, it was now very obvious that they wanted justice, and were more than willing to help out with answering questions or calling to report suspicious activity. Once again, public trust became such a norm that it was too easy to serve the public, nothing was seen as a barrier, and people were starting to see the police as good guys, not the prejudiced stereotype that had been painted of them prior to the Rapalo incident. Wayne was on a new path of enlightenment that had him smiling every day, and the public, from the point of Rapalo's arrest, was never viewed in a conspicuous fashion. Public relations had successfully reduced the criminal activity in the Miami-Dade area, and the re-thinking of policing strategies became more common than any other time that Wayne, as well as many other law enforcement officers, had considered. Community policing and problem-solving methods were again starting to be reconsidered, and at this point there was a general consensus by both the public and police departments that these types of methods could be successfully implemented and sustained. New community organizations were developed and, with the support of law enforcement and other public officials, soon spread like a wildfire in the Shenandoah area. The terrible incidents that had occurred for over a year had birthed something amazing in the area; researchers and other law enforcement specialists were arriving in the Miami-Dade area to observe what was going on, as well as to see how their careers could be enhanced.

The small Shenandoah district had gone from the country's worst eyesore with regard to law enforcement to the ideal example of how a community should be structured. Wayne's faith had reestablished his thoughts about how something had entered his community for a reason and that its purpose was greater than anyone could ever expect. Most importantly, Wayne's dedication to the Rapalo case, the arrest of the Shenandoah Rapist, and the collective efficacy that had ensued began to open doors for him. His newly acquired phone had been bombarded with voicemails that asked him to conduct other media interviews that had a national audience. His partner was receiving the same attention, and both he and Wayne were excited about being able to be seen as celebrities in the law enforcement profession. The interviews were scheduled, and television appearances would soon be broadcasted to the entire nation. Wayne and his partner knew that this was going to be the attention that was necessary, would be desired by any police commissioner, and would provide not only more personal opportunities, but also a technique that could make police officers throughout the world look like heroes. It was time to let the world know that the police were serving, protecting, permanently and remove any cynical perspectives that had been spoken or thought.

Chapter Six

NEW BEGINNINGS

—✺—

Wayne knew that his press conference after Ralapo's second arrest was televised throughout the entire nation, however, he did not think that it would make such a lasting impression. He expected that it, like most other police conferences, would ride the media waves for a few days, and then everything would return to the way it was before the interviews. Wayne was certainly proven wrong about this. His phone had met its capacity because of the previously mentioned voice messages, so much of his day centered on returning phone calls and scheduling interviews with both local and national media. It appeared that everyone wanted to speak to the guys who were responsible for saving the Miami-Dade area from suffering an extended length of despair. The local media started the Wayne Cox hype and then bounced the interviews and knowledge to the more well-known media outlets in the United States. This, in turn, made Wayne and his partner much more recognized in the community and law enforcement world, which only added to their already established prosperity.

MSNBC RIGHT NOW   11:06 PT
DET. WAYNE COX
MIAMI-DADE POLICE DEPT.
FROM SMALL ARMS FIRE DURING COMBAT OPERA' NAS 19.56

As previously mentioned, once the local media interviews were conducted, Wayne and his partner were invited to the more prominent television shows. This made the two quite nervous, but also very excited to be able to represent their department in such a fashion. Wayne and his partner were instructed again on what information could be discussed, which mostly included the typical lines about how the manhunt was a team effort and the victims were the true heroes. Nonetheless, many of the questions were very general. The media wanted to hear about what the evil carbon-based life form did during his reign of terror, how he managed to escape from jail, and what the encounter was like when Wayne and his partner approached Rapalo.

Wayne found this to be surprising, because not many of the media people were thinking in terms of how this rapist had hurt eleven females, as well as how he managed to instill an enormous amount of fear into the community. Yet he went forth with the process of the questioning, and in a short period of time, he became an icon for victim's rights groups and other advocacy organizations. His supervisors and other colleagues seemed to enjoy his innate skills while in front of the camera as well; Wayne's ability to be calm and professional in front of a large audience gave law enforcement the marketing strategy that they had been desperately looking for. Additionally, his interviewing skills included Spanish, which was such a desired language that he was internationally recognized by Hispanic and Latino activists.

All over the Miami-Dade area Wayne was making headlines, and even popping up in world-renowned newspapers and magazines. People as far away as Los Angeles and New York City knew about Wayne and his partner's encounter with the Shenandoah Rapist, but all of these awards came at a cost. Wayne was starting to the think negatively again. His mind started to initiate thoughts about how he, his partner, and his department were all reaping the benefits of such a terrible course of events, and the victims were receiving little, if any, attention other than the help from professionals who specialized in some form of trauma. Wayne was now reading and watching headlines that had him and his partner as the main source of attention, and was starting to wonder if this would hinder the upcoming trial that Rapalo would soon face. He knew that Rapalo was going to be found guilty, but his thoughts were centered on how when he took the witness stand, or entered the courtroom, the victims and their families would view him as a terrible leech who had profited from their heinous experiences.

In a new state of mind, Wayne learned to discuss his emotions better with the people who surrounded him. His partner was the first to catch wind of the depressing thoughts that Wayne was enduring, but others suggested that he had been overanalyzing his experiences, too, and that he may be experiencing post-traumatic stress as well. After discussing his thoughts with his family and supervisors, there was a general consensus that Wayne should seek help elsewhere. Wayne took the advice of his colleagues and soon found himself spiritually engaged in meditation and prayer. The insight he received calmed his self-loathing thoughts, and Wayne was then able to better prepare for the upcoming trial that he had to participate in. Still, the interviews and other media requests were pouring in, and he enjoyed the attention; after all, he did feel as if he deserved some positivity in his life after all that had occurred in the year that Rapalo terrorized his community.

The date for Rapalo's trial was approaching, and Wayne felt more confident about entering that environment and being able to control his emotions. He reassured himself with thoughts that his interviews and media appearances had done nothing to personally hinder the victims, and his partner and other friends supported the train of thought. However, the strength of the guilt got to him the night before he was supposed to appear in court, and Wayne's rewards from other peoples' tragedies made him toss and turn all night long. The morning was not any better, because Wayne burned his breakfast and spilled his coffee. Everything seemed to be going wrong for him so far, and he knew that he had to pull it together in order to professionally represent his department and show the world how justice was supposed to be served.

CHAPTER SEVEN

REWARDS OF STRESS

———⚬⚬⚬———

S o much time had elapsed since Rapalo's second arrest that Wayne was not only worried about his insecure thoughts, but also about whether he had been properly prepped for the trial that was about to take place. He had been in the spotlight for recapturing Rapalo and was able to cash in on other media appearances due to the craziness of Rapalo actually having the nerve to request bail and a change of venue for false claims of police abuse. While arriving at the courthouse, Wayne was not as digressive as he was earlier, and his motivation to do the right thing kicked in again. However, while walking into the building, something reestablished his guilty conscience about how his rewards had come at the expense of the victims' suffering. A security officer said, "I'll bet you be on T.V. even more after today." When Wayne heard this, his stomach dropped, and a hot flash entered his body. Wayne knew that there was some truth in the remark, and that he would most likely be invited to discuss the events in more depth after each day of the trial, and even more so after the long-awaited sentence had been given.

Guilt entered his mind at the most inappropriate time. Wayne had to use the restroom prior to taking the witness stand, before supplying the jury, victims, attorneys, and journalists who were desperately awaiting his nail-in-the-coffin testimony. The time had come, and Wayne could feel all the eyes staring at him as he took the famous oath of truth and sat in the tiny witness box. He could not help but direct his attention to Rapalo and notice the smirk on his face. Even worse, he made the mistake of making a glance at the eleven year-old girl who was scheduled to testify and face her assailant.

The prosecutor was the first to ask Wayne about his encounter with the rapist. Detective Cox was surprised at how easy the questions were. All that was required was basically a review of that particular night. This was not a problem for Wayne because it was the most important day in his life, and he remembered every minute's detail. Then came the cross-examination by Rapalo's representative, and before the man had asked Wayne any questions, he gave him an eye-slanted look that was comprehended without words. His eyes directed him to the young girl that was sitting in the courtroom, but the attorney refused to acknowledge the despair that Wayne was attempting to show. During this line of questioning, Wayne had to refrain from screaming at the defense for sinking so low that he could actually represent such a low-life scumbag and suggest that he was responsible for the final struggle that left him and Rapalo with scratches and bruises. All in all, Rapalo did run away and resist, and, most importantly, he was identified through scientific evidence that showed he was the person responsible for the vicious rapes.

Stress began to emanate further when Wayne was relinquished from his testimony. It was time for the innocent eleven-year-old girl to take the stand and not only be questioned, but face the evil spirit who had committed unspeakable acts upon her. Wayne's foot and leg were bouncing up and down as she took the same oath that he did and sat down in the same chair. At first, her voice cracked and had a tone of wariness that everyone expected. Then something happened that could only be explained by Wayne's faith in his Higher Power. The young girl made eye contact with Wayne, and at that moment, he felt the same feelings that he had felt when he was chasing and wrestling with Rapalo. Then Wayne's mind manifested the words that he had repeated when he was entangled with the evilest spirit to ever enter the Shenandoah district: "God can do great things for those who believe." This wisdom was transferred to the young girl with Wayne's simple nod of the head and confident expression. Somehow—using a power that Wayne believes to be larger than this Earth—she understood this without proper communication. Immediately, she began to answer the questions with superb confidence and vocabulary that no average eleven-year-old would know.

This testimony blew Wayne's time in the hot seat out of the water, and the entire courtroom was filled with the anguish and ideas of justice that were needed to move forward with this criminal proceeding. Wayne believed in due process, but after hearing the story and testimony of the young girl, he could not help but think of historical forms of torture. Although his anger was settled and he focused on the light that was shining on the young girl, her braveness and will to show the world what she had endured made Wayne's prior resentments toward his life and profession seem extremely minor in comparison. His paranoid thinking about all the benefits he had received because of the serial rapes ended when he watched this girl take a stand against evil, and he now knew that his interviews and plans for joining and initiating advocacy groups for such a cause were more than righteous.

The awards from the stress that came from others became not as burdening after that day in the trial, and after eleven life sentences were given to Rapalo, notions of moving on entered Wayne's mind. He was starting to believe that there was more to life than conducting interviews and prospering economically, but this mentality was again challenged when he spoke to more victims at one of the organizations where he had volunteered, and the idea that he had been chosen by a Higher Power to be the voice for the many people who could not speak about their victimization was reaffirmed. The challenge became bigger than representing his department and law enforcement colleagues. Wayne was now taking on interviews and participating in meetings that had monumental significance attached to them, but because he was true to his profession and community, he always put Rapalo's crimes and the victims' experiences at the forefront of any of the conversations.

He was now embracing the rewards that had come his way, but because of his newfound success, his mind generated unprecedented insecure thoughts again. With all of the turmoil that ensued, and with the relief that reaffirmed his dedication and activities, Wayne was now, for the first time in his life, asking questions about why he was the one who had this unusual life experience. Why was it him and not the detective who had come across Rapalo's cases many times? What was it that Wayne did to deserve such a life? Was he chosen by something that had predetermined his fate? Wayne was now forced to deal with an entirely different approach to his successes, and he knew that this might be something that no specialist or medical doctor could help him with.

CHAPTER EIGHT

WHY ME?

S eeking answers for this strange purpose was more difficult than Wayne had expected, but his detective skills set
in and he found himself engaging in a new investigation. He
had comprehensive questions about himself and how or why
he had been selected to have these occurrences happen to him.
Questions about his and every other being's purpose had arisen
before in Wayne's life, but not to the extent where he was constantly dwelling on them or going as far as speaking to religious leaders about these unexpected life events. Searching for
results also entered his mind as he was performing media interviews; Wayne found himself staring at the interviewer and cameras at times, wondering about how these people and devices
were somehow important and how they could leech onto him
and create sustained employment from his work. Nevertheless,
Wayne left these philosophical thoughts to the side and conducted himself in a professional manner; he knew that not

only was he generating an audience for his newly acquired endeavors, but he was giving his department the attention that they truly deserved.

Weeks turned into months, and Wayne was still being contacted by media corporations; at one point, a short film was made about the "Real Miami Vice" and the Rapalo arrest. Wayne's thought about why he was chosen started to fade away. As he continued his old and new routines, not many signals were found that explained why he had encountered such an unusual course of events in his life. "Why me?" had turned into "I can't figure it out so move on," and not much was giving Wayne hope for figuring out the biggest question in his life that he had ever asked himself. Every situation or possible path had been taken, and Wayne was now fixed on the idea that he should move on with his life and not dwell on the past.

Wayne's position where his community, family, and friends were able to communicate effectively with him and not deal with the old version of Wayne was too much to lose. He did not want to be selfish again or take anything away from the relationships that he had worked so hard to redeem. Thoughts about why he was chosen for this mission still percolated in his mind, and the desire to answer this question was becoming stronger as he carried on with his life. The monkey on his back had returned, but this time it was not the pressure from solving a string of terrible crimes; the investigation's purpose was solving the issues of the investigator, an obstacle that seemed impossible to resolve.

More time had passed and the media attention was dying out, so Wayne figured that this may be the best time to try to look deeper into the question that had plagued his mind for so long. The first step was understanding his faith better; Wayne began to read scripture and attended religious assemblies more than he had in the past. As his knowledge about his faith expanded, the answer to the question was still far out of reach. Therefore, he decided to take a different approach and began to subtly pose questions to his friends and family. This method also failed, as the answers were usually ended up a reassuring shoulder rub and short chit-chat that only entertained ideas about how Wayne was thinking too deeply about everything. Progress was not being made at all. Investigating himself stumped Wayne more than anything else he had ever dealt with. Religious texts, conversations, and attending particular meetings had done nothing to help Wayne understand why he had been given this life. Rapalo was arrested and sentenced, but the fact remained that he was still controlling Wayne's mind. Wayne thus devised a plan that seemed to be both crazy and logical. He was considering risking his professional stature and breaking numerous codes of conduct by speaking directly to the man who had caused all of the chaos in the town, and more importantly caused his unsettled thoughts. Seeking out Rapalo was nothing to jump right into, so Wayne decided to think about this idea for several days; he pondered about which question he should ask and how to go about asking them. Wayne even considered asking the question he had been stuck with, "Why me," but he knew that Rapalo probably did not have an answer, and if he did, then it was likely that not much would be settled by the pleasure that Rapalo might get from seeing the man who had arrested him being so distraught and fixated on a complex issue.

More sunrises and sunsets elapsed. Wayne had this question at the front of his mind; it was time to make a decision that would change his life for the better again, end his career, or change the type of Wayne Cox stories that appeared in the media. Of course he was skeptical about going to speak with Rapalo. The code of conduct that his supervisors had given him was going to be broken, and Wayne did not want to draw any more negative attention to the Shenandoah district, the department, or the Miami-Dade area. He thought about headlines saying he had been fired or disobeyed his supervisors entered his mind. Punchy lines like "Cox fired for insubordination," or, "Cop Who Caught Rapalo Gone Rogue," scared Wayne to the point that he began to feel intimidated not by seeking the answer for his question, but by blowback that may occur if he were to go through with such a course of action.

This dilemma had gotten the best of Wayne, and he now wanted to end it; the collateral damage was a secondary inconvenience when compared to finding out why he was chosen to deal with these criminal matters. Even worse, Wayne knew that Rapalo may not even be able to help him, but he still felt compelled to go speak to him to see if some sense could be found about why he was not only the one who arrested Rapalo, but also the person who had the spotlight shined on him after-wards as well. The morning that Wayne had worked up a sufficient amount of confidence to go see Rapalo was not the burst of sunshine that he wanted it to be. The sky was gray and wet and the air was heavy with guilt, but he was still going to go through addressing a conversation with the man who had created his glory.

Upon arriving at the facility, Wayne flashed his badge and made it seem like he was conducting official police business, but in his heart he knew that the investigation was over and this was only a personal interview. All of the correctional officers were giving him strange looks, and were not sure how to view the tasks that had come before them. Wayne's celebrity-like status projected a hint of arrogance even though he was not that type of person. Some of the law enforcement professionals in his town hated him because he was put on a pedestal and no longer considered the typical doughnut-eating and coffee-drinking police officer. Nevertheless, they made the calls and told Wayne where to sit. The time it took for Rapalo to make it to the floor where Wayne was, felt like an eternity. Between the time Wayne arrived and the time Rapalo appeared a few feet across from him, it started to seem like this visit was an ill-conceived idea.

Wayne began to hear the radio calls and other sounds of the team of correctional officers that were assigned to watch Rapalo getting louder. Then, the door locks made noises, and Wayne found himself staring at the evil spirit that he had encountered not too long before. The court appearance was what Wayne remembered the most, and, more specifically, the smirk that Rapalo had when he and the young girl had testified against him. Rapalo looked worn out, but also excited to see his capturer again; a smile radiated from his greasy pale face, and Wayne could feel that tingling sensation again with every step that Rapalo took toward the empty chair across from him. Wayne's body felt cold and frozen when Rapalo sat across from him, and he was confused about how to start the conversation.

He started off with a simple question because he thought that this was the best approach to calm his worried mind. "Do you remember me?"

Rapalo answered with a short and cocky "Yes." Rapalo sat there without going into detail or prompting any other kind of rapport.

Wayne knew that he had to lighten up the mood to keep from caving to the evil spirit's power and hindering his reason for being there. He posed an open question which required more than a single word answer: "Tell me, what's on your mind?"

Rapalo answered without any hesitation. He said that he was mad about Wayne and his partner chasing him and being arrested. He felt no remorse or guilt about the rapes and damage that he caused. Again, Wayne was starting to think that this interview was a terrible idea. The coldness that he was feeling was starting to take over until he remembered the words that had helped on so many similar situations before. Wayne became angry because he knew that he was again letting Rapalo control his life and mind, but this all changed when he repeated the words in his mind: "God can do great things for people who believe." It was as if a switch had been turned on, and Wayne was now poised, with the confidence and motivation that was much needed at this point.

The conversation was over, and Wayne was now engulfed with the same warming sensation that he had felt the night that Rapalo was arrested as well as during the courtroom appearances. His next choice of words was a statement, not a question. Wayne was very direct and asked Rapalo why he had thought Wayne was the one who had arrested and chased him down. Rapalo looked into Wayne's eyes and smirked once again, and replied with a short answer that devastated Wayne: "Luck, pure luck." This was not the lengthy answer that Wayne was expecting, and to his further dismay, the three word reply left him with more questions and confusion about the purpose of this experience. Looking at the group of correctional officers, Wayne signaled with a head nod that he was done with Rapalo. Not long after the talk had started, it was over. Not much of what Wayne wanted to do was accomplished.

Crushed by Rapalo's arrogance, Wayne began to leave the jail and walk to his car. Then he noticed something that was remarkable and could be a possible act from his higher power. The temperature was warmer, and the sky was no longer gray. Wayne took this as a sign that what he had just done was necessary in order for him to move on with his life. He tried to dismiss this notion at first by suggesting to himself that it was later in the day and the sun had merely risen a bit more, but then another sign crossed his path. He noticed two young Hispanic females speaking to one another on the sidewalk. One was obviously a mother, and the other was her daughter, who resembled the eleven year-old to whom Wayne had spoken during his investigation. This girl was not her, but she looked a lot like her. Then something astonishing occurred: the young girl had noticed that Wayne was looking, and she suddenly stopped and waved to him, as well as saying "Hi, Wayne!" The idea that he had become a role model for a young girl was something that had never crossed his mind. After a few seconds after disbelief about the fact that the girl knew who he was, he decided that it was surely time to move on with his life.

THE MIAMI HERALD | MiamiHerald.com
METRO & STATE

CORRECTIONS

Jail raid reunites cop with rapist

■ Miami-Dade detective Wayne Cox saw a familiar face during a jail inspection; a serial rapist he helped capture.

BY DAVID OVALLE
dovalle@MiamiHerald.com

During an inspection of Miami-Dade County Jail this week, Detective Wayne Cox saw a surprising face from his past.

Inside a cell: Reynaldo E. Rapalo, the convicted serial rapist who last year staged a Hollywood-style jail bust only to be caught six days later by Cox and another detective.

"It was surreal. It felt like time froze and it was happening all over again," said Cox, a Miami-Dade police narcotics detective.

Rapalo "freaked out," Cox recalled, but the two chatted amiably through the bars for about 12 minutes.

"He was still a little upset I caught him," Cox said.

Rapalo, dubbed Miami's Shenandoah Rapist, is awaiting transfer to state prison, where he'll serve consecutive life sentences for his crimes.

Coincidence brought Cox, of the Tactical Narcotics Team, to the jail's sixth-floor on Monday.

UNLIKELY MEETING: During a jail raid, Detective Wayne Cox, right, spotted convicted rapist Reynaldo E. Rapalo, left, whom he arrested last year.

He and other Miami-Dade detectives, as well as corrections guards, staged a surprise raid on three jail floors. They confiscated half a gram of cocaine, 24 illegal pills and two homemade knives.

"Those two shanks could have been used to stab a corrections officer," said Miami-Dade Maj. Charles Nanney.

Last December, Rapalo escaped from the Turner Guilford Knight Correctional Center using ropes fashioned from bed sheets.

His escape sparked one of the largest manhunts in recent history and a massive upheaval in Miami-Dade's corrections department.

Six days after Rapalo escaped, a tip took detectives Cox and Alcides Velez to a shopping center at the intersection of Bird Road and Southwest 67th Avenue.

Rapalo, sporting a pink boa, initially gave Cox a fake name and claimed he was a homeless Nicaraguan.

After a brief chase, Rapalo was caught.

Nearly a year later, Rapalo displayed his usual dark charm when he saw Cox, the detective said.

Said Cox: "I guess he thought it was funny."

CHAPTER NINE

MOVING ON

———

S tarting a second life was demanding as Wayne recognized his family was now his number one priority, yet
also had goals he desired to accomplish. Juggling his media
interviews was another challenge since he did not want to
take too much on at one time. Still, the mental excursions
that he was once having were now over, and Wayne was
again engaging in a lifestyle that was full of delight and
wonderful people. At this point in his life, he could truly say
that he had moved forward and was no longer thinking negatively; the cynicism that he once felt seemed to have disappeared completely. Wayne was going to make every minute
of his life enjoyable.

His vitality was noticed everywhere he went and, in
return, opened more doors for him. These opportunities
allowed for the continuance of his growth. Wayne had accomplished what he wanted. His mind seldom reverted to the old

way of thinking and feeling prior to and during the investigation that forever changed his life. However, this retroactive thinking was a tool that Wayne used so that he could appreciate his new outlook on life. Rapalo was now seen as the evil person he was. Wayne would not let the terrible actions of a delinquent person run his life. He also reminded himself of the victims and how their lives had changed. Images of the eleven-year-old girl's testimony always superseded Wayne's negative thoughts. Post-traumatic stress was not a diagnosis that Wayne would allow. He knew that he was not suffering from pressure because of the Rapalo incidents anymore, and, in fact, he was quite happy and not undermined by the experiences that he had endured.

His effort in the advocacy groups joined were also starting to pay off in the manner that he had anticipated. Wayne did not join these groups to bolster his popularity and wasn't a public relations movement. He truly wanted to help people, and his choice to continue to work in law enforcement only verified this. Victims began to see Wayne as a person who they could turn to for help, and some of them even went as far as seeking assistance by asking him to explain how he felt during all of the craziness that Rapalo had created. Because of this, his professional network nearly doubled, and Wayne was now a merited community leader when not working as a police officer.

Everything was going well for Wayne including his determination to move forward with life not allowing his prior emotions or disturbing investigations to take over. Yet he also used them to remind himself how they helped him become a better individual; nothing from this point was going to hinder Wayne's independence or happiness. He was not afraid to admit that the times when he was down allowed him to have an enviable perspective on life. Advancing forward with his life was the best choice he could have made. He had been through it all, from questioning his profession, faith, and understanding of the world, to embracing it being able to see how everything was an opportunity to enhance his well-being. Wayne was not sure what life had in stored for him next but, whatever he had coming his way was from a higher power he confide in.

Wayne still resides in the Miami-Dade area with his two children, continuing his duties as a detective in the Vice Department. He is grateful for the opportunity to advocate for victims of rape and other crimes, and most importantly, his joy still remains. Detective Cox and his partner consider themselves to have more than a professional relationship. Their families are very close with one another spending much of their free time and holiday seasons surrounded by each other. Wayne continues to conduct media appearances and explains how his life was changed by the terrible tragedies that occurred. Nonetheless, his time as a law enforcer is getting closer to its end. He plans on rejuvenating his career by living out the majority of his life with the same passions and reasons that he took his job as a police officer—to serve and protect the community.

As for the Shenandoah district and Miami-Dade area, it has maintained the state that it entered after Rapalo was captured for the second time. Wayne and the rest of the law enforcement community are still seen as a group that is dedicated to helping others, and the Rapalo incident is now viewed almost as a necessary evil that brought such a form of collective worth to their community. The majority of the residents will contribute the prevalence of happiness to having good people in the community. Wayne and the Shenandoah district, believe in their hearts that this terrible period of time did allow for them to reach out to one another and form an impervious bond. Each of the victims have carried on with their lives to the best of their abilities and are aware that they have the complete support of the people in the Shenandoah district, the law enforcers, and especially from Detective Cox.

Finally, Wayne believes that his "Why me" question was answered, and that God put him through this experience because he knew that Wayne would take the information and lessons that were learned and educate many others on the subject matter. To Wayne, this was the method God had devised in order to show him his true calling in life. Wayne was not concerned with money or fame. His media interviews were another strategy that he deployed in order to help as many people as possible. Wayne became even more specific about the answer to his question as he began educating women and children, and he even implemented this philosophy into his media appearances. He is currently fully involved in victims' advocacy work, and even teaches at many places so that individuals will be able to identify the behaviors of people like Rapalo. His work and dedication is recognized all over the world. Many victims, and their families look to him for inspiration and guidance. Wayne respects the people who have encountered such a traumatic experience, and will do anything in his power to assist them.

He has become a great educator on the behavior of sexual predators for law enforcement as well. Many agencies now turn to him for advice or training pieces so that other individuals can serve, protect, and identify the behaviors of sexual assailants. Being a faith-based person, Wayne allows God to guide him in the direction that permits him to help as many people as possible. To say that nothing good came from the Rapalo's crimes is far from being logical. Wayne's desire to evade the rights of the citizens to be violated has helped him to conduct himself in a religious and professional manner. Detective Cox undeniably developed inner growth through this experience. Yet he is far from becoming the man the Lord would like for him to be. Life's lessons will continue to challenge him in an effort to provide him with increasing knowledge. The knowledge he will passionately share with others.

AUTHOR

Detective Wayne Cox was born in New York City. During his childhood years he moved to Jamaica with his family permitting him the opportunity to cherish his origins first hand. Although living in Jamaica was pleasant, the family relocated to Miami, Fl. with new goals. In Miami, Detective Cox spent the remainder of his young adult years growing to love a community he would unknowingly later protect.

Det. Cox earned a B.S. in Criminal Justice from Florida International University while effectively working as a Miami Dade County Officer. During the last twenty years Det. Cox has served his community through the Tactical Narcotics Team (TNT), Warrants Bureau Felony Division, Community Oriented Policing Services (COPS) and the Port of Miami. Throughout the five years he contributed to the TNT force his hard work was highly commended by the Mayor, Commissioners and citizens of Miami Dade County for the recapture of the Shenandoah rapist. Interviews pertaining to this event from CNN, CNBC, Fox News and other media are available for viewing at Wayne Cox The Real Miami Vice–You Tube www.youtube.com/watch?v=M45Hvr3tGl4

As a member of the TNT unit he infiltrated the dangerous world of prostitution, narcotics, human trafficking and money laundering. His TNT unit had the privilege of training the Miami Vice movie cast members including the lead stars Colin Farrell and Jamie Fox. By means of this event Det. Cox received the nickname "Tubbs" on the streets of Miami. His elite Tactical Narcotics Team was also imitated by Hollywood's Block Buster Movie Bad Boys II featuring Will Smith and Martin Lawrence. The movie used as reference the Miami Dade Police Department's TNT unit Det. Cox operated with.

Detective Cox also dedicated four years to the Warrants Bureau Felony Division. In this position he pursued fugitives within the United States with violations consisting of murder, robbery, narcotics, and rape subjects. He conducted duties responsible for the safety of the airplane as he escorted these high profile offenders with the support of respected Air Marshals to their jurisdiction. Det. Cox also devoted five years to specific low-income based communities. During his years in the Community Oriented Policing Services (COPS) Det. Cox established trust among the people and great friendships. He found pleasure in assisting government officials as they utilized resources to target problems among these communities. Continuing to search for growth, Det. Cox transferred to the Port of Miami Division. He has the privilege of working with the FBI, customs border patrol, the coast guard and homeland security. The Port of Miami is one of the largest cargo container ports in the United States and accounts for 4.3 million passengers each year consequently being a high targeted area. Det. Cox takes great pride in protecting the welfare of the passengers as well as the Port of Miami from any terrorist attacks.

Detective Cox continues to reside in Miami Dade County dedicating his leisure time to the community as an advocate. The years of involvement in Law Enforcement have prepared him for this new chapter in his life. Working as a member of each unit provided him with the knowledge needed to pursue a more difficult challenge. With the Lord's direction each unit's experience became a link to a path of research and finally definite results. He strongly believes that his website www.encounterwitharapist.net can prevent both sexual assault on children and women in this country. As stated in his website our society needs to establish programs to educate our kids about sexual predators. Knowledge is power, let's give our kids a fighting chance.